ZEN SCIENCE

Stop and Smell the Universe

The Institute of Zen Science

RUNNING PRESS

PHILADELPHIA

INDTRODUCTION

"The most beautiful thing we can
experience is the mysterious."
—Albert Einstein

This is a book of science facts
that are also Zen meditations.

They're meant to be read one at a time, savored, and
then used as tools to experience the paradox of who
we are in the universe—how we're both big and small
. . . solitary and connected . . . ephemeral and eternal.
When you look in a mirror, feel your feet on the
ground, gaze at a flower, or stare at the sky, we hope
you'll be able to retrieve these facts and use them to
experience a sense of connection to all things; to see
past the illusions of the material world and live more
fully in the moment.

"The true purpose of Zen is to see things as
they are, to observe things as they are, and
to let everything go as it goes."
—Shunryu Suzuki, Zen master

There are a lot of numbers in this book, because quantifying things is a key part of science. But don't get hung up on the numbers. We've tried to be accurate with them, but the truth is, they're really a moving target. Years ago, for example, scientists estimated there were 200 billion galaxies in the universe; now they estimate two trillion. That's a huge disparity—so which is correct? We don't know . . . and it's reasonable to assume that the estimate will change again. But philosophically it really makes no difference. Either way, the point is to know that the universe is inconceivably vast . . . and we are part of it. That applies to most of the information included here as well. The details may change, but the larger message is constant.

And by the way, don't be fooled by the casual way we use the terms millions, billions, and trillions. Most of us understand what a million is and then we sort of naturally think of billions as "bigger" and trillions as "even bigger." But philosophically, we lose a lot with that kind of thinking. A million seconds is slightly more than eleven days. A billion seconds is about 32 years, and a trillion seconds is about 32,000 years. As one observer puts it: "The difference between a billion and trillion is equivalent to the difference between your lifetime and the entirety of human history." To get the most out of this book, keep that sense of perspective.

At their hearts, Zen and science have this in common: illumination. We hope this material adds a little bit of wonder, joy, illumination, and fulfillment to your life.

Earth is not our planet.

We think of it as ours, but for 99.9994 percent of Earth's existence—virtually all of it—there have been no human beings on the planet.

Scientists believe Earth formed some 4.6 billion years ago, and the first single-celled life-forms appeared about 800 million years later. The first dinosaurs appeared 230 million years ago, and they flourished for 160 million years before going extinct. It's estimated that our oldest primate ancestors appeared just seven million years ago, and that another million years passed before they began walking upright. It wasn't until about 200,000 years ago that our own species, *Homo sapiens*, appeared. So humans have been around less than one-hundredth of 1 percent of the 3.8 billion years that life has existed on Earth.

Cleopatra's breath . . .

. . . is still in the air.

When Cleopatra took her last breath, she exhaled around 100 *sextillion* air molecules—that's 100 followed by 21 zeros—mostly carbon dioxide and nitrogen. So many were dispersed into the atmosphere that they're still floating around . . . everywhere.

What's the result? Every time you inhale, according to experts, you take in at least one molecule that came from Cleopatra's lungs, and Julius Caesar's, and George Washington's. In fact, it's likely that with every breath you take in at least one molecule breathed by every one of your ancestors all the way back to the very first humans who started your family tree.

Inner space

There's more of you than you think.

Right now, your body contains an estimated
two thousand trillion trillion oxygen atoms.
That's more than the total number of leaves in
every forest on Earth.

The paradox of perception

If something feels hot, it's actually getting cooler. If something feels cool, it's actually getting warmer.

Heat naturally flows from a warm to a cold object, until they achieve a balance. An object feels warm because it's losing heat to you; it feels cool because the heat from your body is flowing away from you.

Feel the flow.

Everything around you is moving all the time.

No matter how solid and stationary
something seems, on an atomic level it's
always in motion. Your clothes, your chair,
your cup of coffee, this book—everything is
moving—and at incredible speeds.
How do we know they're moving?
They have a temperature. In fact, that's what
temperature is. When an object's atoms are
moving fast, the object feels hot; when the
atoms move slower, it feels colder.

Are you human?

Of course. But most of the cells
in your body are not.

A human cell carries human DNA, which has
the ability to make new people or parts of
people. Yours has been passed on to you by
your parents . . . and to them by their parents
. . . and to them by their parents . . . and so
on. But scientists currently estimate that
only about 40 percent of you is made up of
these human cells. The rest of you—about 60
percent—is bacteria, viruses, fungi, and single-
celled organisms called archaea. They're not
human. And they're not technically you.
In fact, if you died right now, they'd
still be living.

Dead or alive?

When you look at someone, most of what you see is already dead.

"We are," says one observer, "a living sack of water encased in dead cells, like a tree's bark." Pretty much every external part of you is dead: The hair on your body is dead. So are your fingernails and toenails. So are the outermost 18–23 layers of your skin. Even the outer layer of your eyes is dead; your eyes are constantly regenerating it to keep your vision clear.

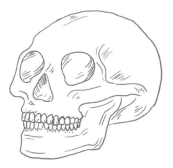

Finding balance

Lightning is more than an awesome show; it keeps our world balanced.

The electrical charges of Earth (negative) and the atmosphere (positive) are balanced perfectly ... but precariously: The planet's electrical charge is constantly flowing into the atmosphere. Fortunately, lightning helps recharge the Earth by striking it 100 times per second. Otherwise, the electrical balance would disappear in five minutes. Scientists don't know what would happen if this balance were upset. The power of lightning keeps us from ever finding out.

At this moment . . .

. . . the entire weight of the atmosphere is resting on your head.

The atmosphere is a giant cushion of air pressing down on our planet and everything on it . . . including you. Every minute of your life, 15 pounds of air are sitting on every square inch of your body.

That's equivalent to the weight of a small car sitting on your head and shoulders.

Just dust

A shooting star isn't a star.
It's a pebble about the size of an apple pit.

A shooting star is really just a particle of
interplanetary dust that burns up on entering
our atmosphere, emitting a burst of light in
the process. Amazingly, this can happen some
20–30 million times *a day* . . . but we never
know it, because most of the dust particles
are too small for us to see.

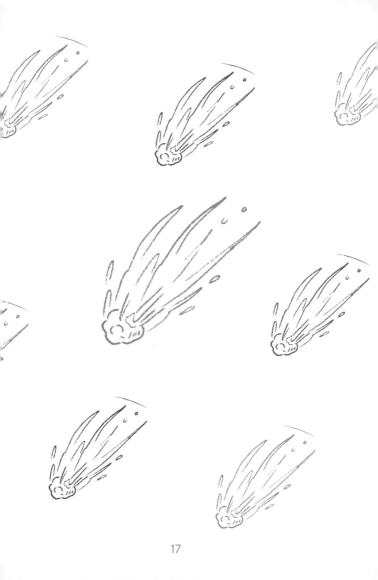

Happy birthday!

You're younger than you think.

You're not the person you were even just a few weeks ago. You can't feel it, but most of the cells in your body are constantly replacing themselves. On average, you grow a new layer of skin every three weeks, new blood every four months, a new liver in a year, a new skeleton in 10 years, and so on. Scientists believe the only cells that remain with you for your entire life are your heart, brain, ovaries, and eyes. The rest of you keeps changing.

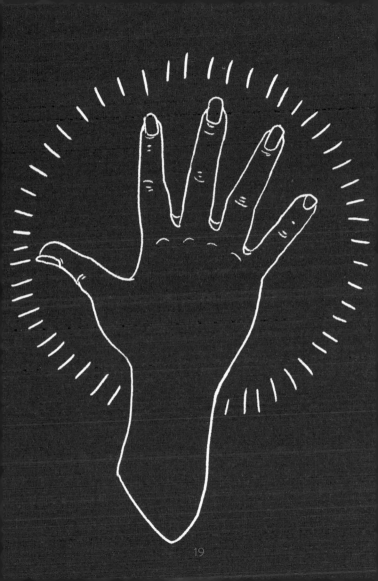

19

Balancing act

You're continually falling as you walk.

No matter how steady you think you are, every time you take a step, you're actually falling forward . . . or backward . . . or to the left . . . or to the right. You don't notice it because your body automatically adjusts your stride to place your foot in the direction of the fall. Studies show that because your legs and pelvis are always correcting your fall, every step you've ever taken has been slightly different than the previous ones.

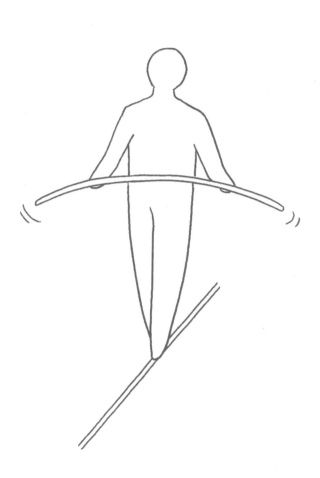

You . . .

. . . contain 60,000 miles of blood vessels.

That's enough to circle Earth
at the equator 2.5 times.

Snap your fingers . . .

More than 3,000 stars were just born.

According to astronomers' estimates, more
than 14 billion stars are born every day. You'll
never see any of them, though, because
they're so far away that you and everyone
else on the planet will be long dead by the
time their light reaches Earth.

How big . . .

. . . is a snowflake?

The average snowflake is estimated at about the size of a penny. But that little bit of ice is made up of 100,000,000,000,000,000,000 water molecules. That's 100 *quintillion*.

To give you an idea of how many that is: if a penny-sized snowflake actually *were* a penny, 100 quintillion of them laid out flat like a carpet would cover the entire surface of the Earth *70 times*.

You're going
in circles . . .

. . . with no destination.
But you're going there fast.

Since the moment you were born, you've
been spinning at 1,000 miles per hour,
orbiting the Sun at 67,000 miles an hour and
orbiting the galaxy at 515,000 miles per hour.
You're doing it now.

And you'll be doing it until the
moment you die.

Atomic world

Look at the period at the end of this sentence.

It's so huge that at least 500 billion atoms
can fit inside it.

29

Beyond your senses

Air is moving all around us. We just can't see it
. . . the same way fish can't see water.

You can feel air in a breeze because trillions
of oxygen and nitrogen molecules are
bombarding your body. But you can't see
it. That's lucky, because if you could, you
wouldn't be able to see anything else.

Why is air "invisible"? We see things because
light reflects off them. But most air molecules
are so small and spread apart that light
easily passes through them with little to no
reflection.

Watch a burning candle.

Do you see the diamonds?

A candle's flame is so hot that it constantly converts carbon atoms in the wax into "nanodiamonds"—diamonds so tiny that humans can't see them. While you're watching it burn, your candle is creating about 1.5 million of them every second.

In the time it takes to read this . . .

. . . around 25 million of your
cells will have died.

Don't worry, though: Before the day is over,
your body will have made more than 300
billion new ones. Living, in a sense, is a balance
between losing cells and creating enough
new cells to replace them. Your body's cells
have life spans just like you. Cell death is an
integral part of our biology (and "death" is
really just the point in time when your cells
stop reproducing).

All one family

You have about as many hairs on your body
as a chimpanzee.

You probably don't think of yourself as
having "fur," but you do. It's just finer than
other animals' fur—so fine, in fact, that
it's almost invisible.

Stand up.

You've just conquered gravity.

We think of gravity as an indomitable force.
And it is powerful . . . but so are you. Every
time you pick up an object, take a step, or
stand, you're overcoming the gravitational
pull of the entire planet. Even a small child
can do it.

Inner space

There's more of you than you might think.

If the atoms in your body were laid end to end, they would go from Earth to the Sun, and back, an estimated five million times.

Measuring the universe

How many stars are there?

- More than the number of seconds that have passed since Earth came into existence.

- More than all the grains of sand on Earth.

- More than all of the words and sounds ever uttered by human beings.

- As many as there are H_2O molecules in 10 drops of water. Yes, really. Scientists estimate that 10 ordinary drops of water contain the same number of molecules as there are stars.

Beyond your senses

Flowers have "runways" and "bull's-eyes" on them that show pollinators where to find food. We just can't see them.

The human eye can only see certain wavelengths of light within what's called the "visible spectrum." Ultraviolet light's wavelength is too short for us to perceive, but bees and other insects can see it. Many flowers that appear plain-looking to us have bold patterns on their petals that are only visible in ultraviolet light. These "runways" on the petals or "bull's-eyes" around the pollen direct insects to the center of the flower, which contains the pollen and nectar they're looking for.

How many . . .

. . . different kinds of plants and animals live on Earth? No one knows.

People discover 15,000 new species every year . . . and we're not even close to finding them all. Scientists believe that as many as 75 percent of all species of plants and animals are still unknown.

Your eyes breathe.

If they didn't, you wouldn't be able to see.

Don't assume you only get oxygen through your mouth and nose. You also "breathe" though your eyes. Normally, your organs get oxygen from your blood. But there are no blood vessels in your cornea . . . so it has to absorb oxygen directly from the air. That's how it stays alive.

Good morning!

Today's sunlight was created
at least 10,000 years ago.

Each particle of light that enters our
atmosphere left the Sun only eight
minutes ago . . . so in a way, it's brand-
new. But it was actually formed in the
core of the Sun between 10,000 and
170,000 years ago. It has been working
its way to the Sun's surface ever since.

Now is then.

Everything you see is already in the past.

Light is the fastest thing in the universe . . .
but it still takes time for it to bounce off
objects and reach our eyes. The farther
the light has to travel, the further back
in time you see.

Consider this: If an alien race on a planet 80
million light-years away used a superpowerful
telescope to look at Earth's surface right now,
they would see dinosaurs.

The paradox of perception

Look in the mirror. You seem solid,
but the truth is, you're mostly liquid.

If you're an average adult, you're 60-70
percent water. The exact amount depends
on how much of your body mass is fat or
muscle. (Fat has less water; muscle has
more water). Babies are about 75 percent
water, and so are potatoes.

For an estimate of how many gallons of
water are in your body, multiply your weight
by 0.65 (the average of 60 and 70 percent),
then divide by 8.4 pounds (the weight of
a gallon of water).

You . . .

. . . were once the youngest person on Earth.

For one instant, at the exact moment of your birth, you had the distinction of being the youngest human in existence, among the billions of living people on the planet.

You're floating.

Your feet never actually touch the ground.

In fact, you never touch anything directly—
and nothing touches you. What you perceive
as physical touch is actually the sensation of
your atoms being repulsed by the atoms of
other objects. The atoms in all matter repel
each other with an electromagnetic force
that's a billion billion billion billion times
stronger than gravity.
Think of magnets whose similar poles push
each other away. That's essentially what's
happening to you and all matter on
Earth . . . all the time.

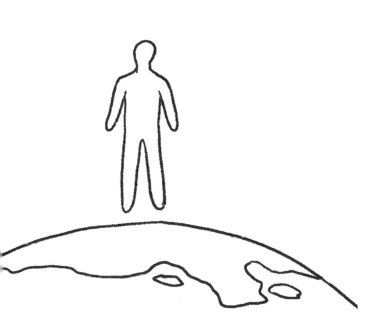

All one family

What do humans and some species of seaweed
have in common?

Answer: Both reproduce using
sperm and eggs.

There's no sex involved (they're plants, not
people), but the bladder wrack—a species
of seaweed—has sperm cells that look
remarkably like ours. Here's how the process
works: The female plants release eggs into the
seawater, which sink to the ocean floor. Then,
when the Moon is full, the male plants release
their sperm. The sperm somehow "know"
to swim away from the moonlight and down
toward the murky depths, where the eggs are
waiting to be fertilized. Many other species of
seaweed reproduce in a similar way.

What's at the center of the Earth?

No one knows for sure.

In school, we were led to believe that scientists knew exactly what's under our feet, all the way to the Earth's core. But those cutaway diagrams teachers showed us were based on analysis of earthquake waves, not on firsthand experience. The deepest anyone has ever drilled into the Earth is 7.5 miles. No one's ever seen anything below that.

Being centered . . .

. . . is not just a spiritual practice. It's the law.

Like everything on the planet, you're being pulled toward one point inside the core of the Earth, called the "center of gravity." This isn't a static point—it keeps moving—so no one is sure exactly where it is at any given moment. We just know it exists, and that all of us—and every thing—are being drawn to it.

You really *are* a star.

You're made of recycled stardust.

About 40 percent of the atoms in your body were created inside stars billions of years ago and then dispersed across the universe when the stars exploded. This stardust was gradually reformed into more stars, planets, solar systems, and eventually . . . you. What about the other 60 percent of your atoms? Those are hydrogen, which came from the Big Bang—about 13.8 billion years ago—before any stars even existed.

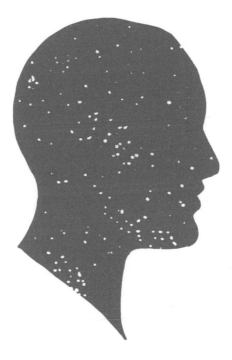

The paradox of perception

Earth's surface seems rough and uneven, but it's actually smoother than a billiard ball.

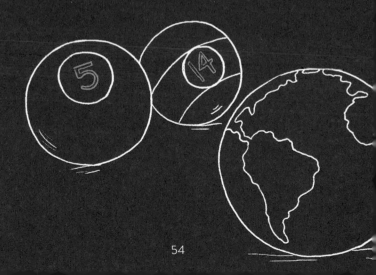

Every billiard ball has to meet certain standards for use in tournaments. If you applied those same standards to a billiard ball the size of Earth, it could have mountains no greater than 17 miles high and low points no deeper than 17 miles below sea level. Now compare that with the real Earth: Mount Everest, its highest point, is 5.5 miles high, and the Mariana Trench, its lowest point, is 6.8 miles deep. So as rough as it may appear to us, Earth is actually *smoother* than a billiard ball.

(But it's not as *round* as a billiard ball. Thanks to centrifugal force caused by its rotation, Earth bulges at the equator.)

You . . .

. . . have a blind spot in each eye,
but your brain conceals it from you.

You probably don't know it, but you're
partially blind. There's a small part of your eye
that has no visual receptor cells. You don't
notice it because your brain uses the visual
data it collects *around* the spot to "fill in" the
missing information. It also uses the data it
receives from both eyes to create a single
mental image, so what one eye misses, the
other often picks up.

At this moment . . .

. . . the atoms in all solid objects (including this book) are making sounds you can't hear.

Every atom in the universe is moving, creating vibrations that can become sound. In 2014, Swedish scientists created an experiment to hear atoms make "the softest sounds physically possible," and they "listened" to an atom. It resonated in the key of D (twenty octaves above the highest note on a piano).

How many . . .

. . . planets are in our solar system?
No one knows.

Despite what they told you in school, we have no idea what's out there. We know that Pluto is some 3.7 billion miles from Earth, but the solar system extends at least another 12 billion miles beyond that, and some scientists suggest it goes a lot farther. So at a minimum, 75 percent of our solar system is still a mystery.

Breathe in . . .

You just inhaled a jungle.

You breathe 12–20 times a minute . . . and in that 60 seconds, you inhale about 300,000 specks of dust—or, if you live in a particularly "grubby" area, probably *millions*. You also inhale an estimated 600 microbes . . . which means you suck in as many as 50 living creatures every time you breathe. But don't panic. Your lungs are built to handle it, and you've been doing it all your life.

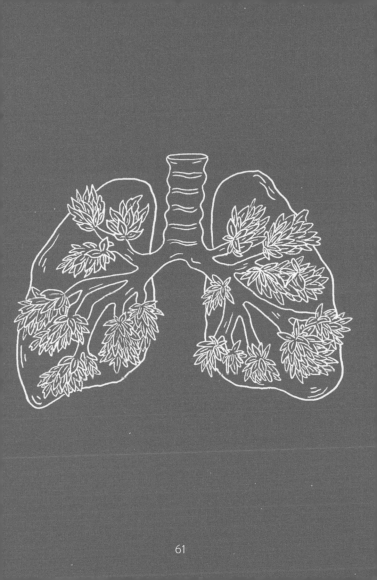

Stop and smell the conversation.

When you smell a flower, you're eavesdropping on an intimate dialogue between plants and pollinators.

A flower can't pursue sexual partners, so it has to attract them with a special language—its scent.

It's not a random conversation; the flower has a specific audience in mind (and knows when to turn on the charm). If its pollinators are active in the daytime, like bees or butterflies, it releases its strongest scent during the day. If the pollinators are nocturnal, like moths or bats, it reserves its best scent for nighttime.

Flowers also "know" that timing is key. They produce fewer odors when they're immature and not yet ready for pollination and emit less-attractive scents after they've been well pollinated. This keeps pollinators focused on more fertile flowers, which helps the species survive.

How old is the rain?

At least three billion years old—maybe older.

Almost all the water that has ever been on
the planet is still here. Our oceans stabilized
three to four billion years ago . . . so all of
Earth's water is at least that old. But scientists
say that between 30 and 50 percent of it is
even older than Earth . . . and also older
than the Sun.

Raindrops form around tiny particles of
dust. Next time you catch a raindrop in your
palm, consider this: Not only is the water
unimaginably ancient, but the particle around
which the raindrop formed may well be meteor
dust left over from when Earth
was formed.

The paradox of perception

A strawberry looks red because it's not red.

Visible light is made of different wavelengths of energy—which we perceive as different colors. When light strikes an object, the object absorbs some wavelengths and "rejects" others. The rejected light waves bounce off the object and hit our eyes. So we see the color that *didn't* become absorbed. The molecules of a strawberry, for example, don't "like" red light, so they reflect it away—but they *do* "like" violet and blue light, so they absorb those waves. That's why strawberries look red to us, even though they're actually more blue-violet. And that's true with pretty much everything we see.

Inner space

There's more of you than you think.

Each one of the 37.2 trillion cells in your body contains a tightly coiled strand of DNA that, if unwound and laid out in a straight line, would be about six feet long. If all 37.2 trillion strands of your DNA were laid end to end, they'd be more than 42 billion miles long. That's more than 15 times the distance between the Sun and Neptune.

We're all floating.

Think about it: There's nothing under our planet.

Earth is suspended in space, held by the gravity of the Sun, the solar system, and the galaxy. No one quite knows what gravity is or why it exists. We just know it's there . . . and it's the reason we're floating.

The universe in your brain

There's more of you than you might think.

Your brain contains 80–100 billion nerve cells—more than 10 times as many as there are humans on the planet. If you add in the number of connections between nerve cells, the sum is about 10,000 times the number of humans who ever lived. One hundred billion is also more or less the same as the number of stars in the Milky Way.

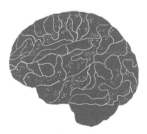

You . . .

. . . are radioactive.

Most of the atoms in your body are stable . . . but not all of them. It's estimated that every second, 9,000 unstable atoms in your body decay, shedding atomic particles and giving off radiation.

The same thing is happening in everything you touch and everything that touches you, including what you eat and drink. One of the most radioactive foods: bananas. Eating 300 of them is roughly the equivalent of having a chest X-ray.

How long is a minute?

Sixty seconds may not seem like a long time to you, yet in a single minute . . .

- A hummingbird can flap its wings 4,000 times.

- At least 10 million new stars are born.

- All of your blood makes a round-trip from your heart to your lungs to the rest of your body and back to your heart.

- About 300 billion gallons of water precipitate around the world. That's about six billion bathtubs' worth.

- You move about 26 thousand million million million molecules of air in and out of your lungs . . . eight times.

You . . .

. . . are 99 percent identical to the person sitting next to you.

Your DNA contains an amazing three billion genetic building blocks, or "base pairs." They make you who you are . . . but they also make everyone else who they are. In fact, no more than 1 percent of you is uniquely you. The rest of "you" is shared with every other human on Earth. (You also share 96 percent of your DNA with chimpanzees.)

Food for thought

Are there universal flavors?

In 2009, astronomers discovered a gas cloud around a newborn star in our galaxy that contains the compound ethyl formate— the chemical responsible for the taste of raspberries and the scent of rum.

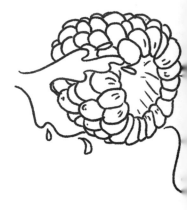

All one family

Take another look at that tiny ant on the ground. It's a lot like you.

Here's a surprise: Humans have an astonishing number of traits in common with ants. For example, ants are farmers—they grow crops of fungi and raise aphids as livestock. (They milk aphids by tickling them with their antennae).

They maintain an organized society with castes and classes; they have armies and launch wars; they have slaves; they make boats; they have community dining areas where they gather to eat; they have bedrooms and cleaning services; and they exchange an endless flow of information. As one scientist describes it: "They do everything but watch television."

The paradox of perception

You actually see the world upside down and backward.

When light enters your eye, the convex shape of your lens flips the image. Result: The image is upside down and reversed when it hits the retina at the back of your eye. That's how you saw the world for the first few days of your life—upside down. But your brain learned to invert the image, and you've been perceiving things "correctly" ever since.

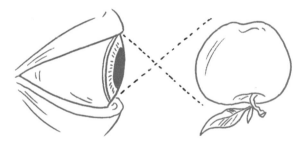

Death

. . . is just the beginning.

After you die—regardless of whether you decompose naturally or are cremated—your body won't turn to dust. Most of it will become air.

The carbon compounds that make up your body will be converted into carbon dioxide and will continue recycling through the land, air, and water for millions of years. Eventually, "you" will float out into space to become part of a star, a meteor . . . or perhaps another life-form on another planet.

The paradox of perception

You think of fire and water as opposites, but actually, fire creates water.

When a candle, a match, or any organic matter burns, it releases carbon and hydrogen. The hydrogen combines with oxygen in the air to make H_2O—water.

Connections

If you like trees, here's good news:
You may be part of one.

If you live close to a tree or walk past one
frequently, there's a good chance that some
of the carbon atoms you've exhaled were
absorbed by the tree . . . and are now part of
the wood, embedded in the rings of its trunk.

Life's size

A teaspoon of soil can contain
a billion living creatures.

There's far more life below the surface of
Earth than above it. Just one spoonful of rich
soil contains more than 4,000 species of
microbes.

Turn your radio on . . .

. . . and you can hear the Big Bang.

When you get static on a radio or TV, about 1 percent of the white noise you hear is left over from the Big Bang. Yes, you can actually listen to the birth of the universe, almost 14 billion years ago. How is that possible? The electromagnetic waves that make the noise started out as very short light waves. They're still with us, but over time, as they've lost energy, they've become longer waves—the type of waves captured by radio and TV antennas. Scientists call this static cosmic microwave background (CMB) because it's everywhere. In fact, it's probably passing through you right now.

Finding balance

It's Earth, not the Sun, that warms the air.

When you feel heat in the air, you probably
assume it comes directly from the Sun. Most
doesn't. About half the heat that reaches
Earth from the Sun is directly absorbed into
the land and oceans. We don't feel it . . . until
Earth radiates it back into the atmosphere.

Breathe in.

You had help.

As one scientist describes it, "the atmosphere breathes for us." All we do is move our chest muscles and diaphragm to make space. Then the weight of the atmosphere *forces* air into our lungs until the pressure is equal to the outside air.

Look up.

A cloud in the sky can weigh a million pounds
. . . yet it floats.

A typical cumulus cloud is more than half a
mile wide and half a mile tall and consists of
about a million pounds of water—roughly the
weight of 100 elephants. So how can it float?
Answer: It's made of trillions of tiny droplets
of water and ice spread out over a huge area.
Some droplets are so tiny that you'd need
millions to make a single raindrop. And they're
so light that gravity has very little effect on
them . . . plus wind and warm updrafts of air
help keep them aloft. But over time, they
combine with other droplets and fall to Earth
as rain or snow.

Do you exist?

Your calculator says no.

Earth's total area is about
5,502,532,127,000,000 square feet.
(That's more than five quadrillion square
feet.) Standing, you only occupy, let's say,
two square feet of it. This is such a small
percentage that the calculator on your
computer is likely to show it as zero.

You're older than you think.

In fact, you're as old as your mother.

Nature has a special way of protecting human eggs: They're formed in a girl while she's still in her mother's womb, and she's born with them. Those eggs remain inside her body until they become viable and can be fertilized. So when your mother was born, she was already carrying you—or at least the egg that became you.
That means your mother's birthday is your birthday too.

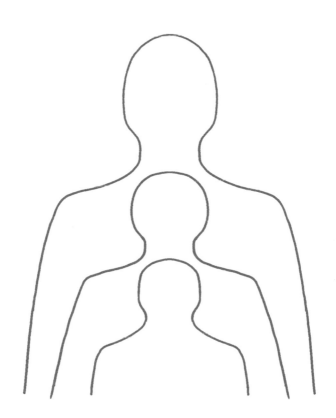

You can't eat sunlight.

But green plants can.

Look at any green plant. You probably see a tree, or a weed, or a blade of grass. Now try to see them for what they really are: factories that convert solar energy into living matter. All human food depends on this process. And if that's not enough, take a breath and ponder this: That same process is responsible for creating all the oxygen in our atmosphere.

Beyond your senses

Smells aren't invisible.
They're just too small for you to see.

Odors are made up of tiny molecules floating in the air. When you inhale them, they latch onto receptors in the back of your nose, which send a signal to your brain that you interpret as smell. This means that when you smell a flower or an onion or a new car, you're actually ingesting miniscule parts of them. That applies to farts, too. . . . . . But don't worry—the molecules aren't absorbed into your bloodstream—usually.

Food for thought . . .

Anything can be food.

You don't think of rocks as food. Yet Earth hosts a whole group of "rock-eaters" called *lithotrophs*—mostly bacteria, single-celled microorganisms called *archaea*, and some fungi.

They get their energy from "eating" sulfur, iron, nitrogen, and hydrogen. And in some cases, they've been found to feed on uranium, arsenic, and mercury. Actually, you're a rock-eater, too, but you only eat one type of rock: salt.

Life's size

There are more cells in your body than there are
galaxies in the known universe.

There are an estimated two trillion galaxies
in the known universe.
You may be only five or six feet tall,
but your body is made up of an estimated
37 trillion cells.

Paradox of perception

When you drink through a straw, it's the weight of Earth's atmosphere—not suction from your lips—that forces liquid into your mouth.

Your straw is full of air—some pushing down from one end, and an equal amount pushing up from the other end. When you suck on it, you remove the air that's pushing down, which creates a vacuum. Meanwhile, the atmosphere is pushing down on the liquid in your glass. When the air is removed from the top of the straw, the liquid rushes into the vacuum . . . which leads straight to your mouth.

Perfect balance

The water cycle is an exquisite example of balance in nature.

Almost all of the water that evaporates from Earth's surface—about 300 trillion gallons per day—returns to Earth in the form of precipitation. This cycle will continue for as long as water exists on Earth.

Once a molecule of water evaporates, it stays up in the air for about 10 days, then falls. Without this quick turnover our oceans would be empty.

Inner space

How big is a postage stamp?

There are about the same number of protons and neutrons in a postage stamp as there are stars in the visible universe.

Breathe out.

You just fed the entire planet.

Breathing in keeps you alive. But breathing out keeps everything *else* alive. The carbon dioxide you exhale may be a waste product to you, but plants need it to create the oxygen and sugars that support nearly all life on Earth. Every day, just by exhaling, you provide enough carbon dioxide to support two mature oak trees.

Touch a plant.

Can it feel you?

When you touch a plant, it sets off a chain reaction in two directions. One reaction is in your fingers—nerves send an electrical wave to your brain telling you what you're feeling. The other is a reaction in the plant. Although they don't have a central nervous system, plants can sense heat and the pressure from your hand. Some plants, like the cocklebur (which dies if you touch it for too long) or the Venus flytrap, have a visible response. But regardless of whether you can see the reaction or not, scientists have proven that plants do respond to touch.

Food for thought

Your ears are part of every meal.

Research indicates that high-pitched sounds
make food taste sweeter, and low-pitched
sounds make it seem more bitter.

A perfect balance

Every day you shed about a million skin cells
...and "invisible" creatures eat them.

It may sound gross, but dead skin falls off your body at the rate of tens of thousands of flakes per minute. It's not wasted, though. Your dead skin is part of the balance of nature, providing a food source for the millions of tiny dust mites that live all over your house.

What's on the bottom of the ocean?

No one knows.

Only 5 percent of the ocean floor has ever been explored. Scientists have made educated guesses about what it's like and what kinds of creatures live there—but they're just guessing. They don't really know what's on the other 95 percent.

Up is down.

When you look at the sky, are you looking up
... or down into the vast emptiness of space?

Actually, there is no absolute up or down.
Your own sense of up and down comes from
two little gyroscopes in your inner ears. Your
brain uses them to determine whether your
body is upright, horizontal, or upside down.
But what's up to you is down to someone on
the other side of the world. And on a larger
scale, space has no "up" and "down" at all.

Food for thought: If you were looking "up"
at someone on the Moon, and they were
simultaneously looking "up" at you on Earth,
which one of you would really be looking up?

Unlimited power

Your brain operates on just 12–20 watts of electricity.

Considering the amount of activity going on up there—with billions of neurons constantly opening and closing—your brain is incredibly energy-efficient. By comparison, the Watson computer, which was designed to simulate human brain activity, uses 20,000 watts. Actually, your entire body functions on around 100 watts of energy—about the same as an average incandescent lightbulb.

Cosmic living room

There are dinosaurs under your couch.

It may seem improbable, but the "dust bunnies" collecting around your house are made of particles from across time and space—everything from your own skin to moondust, meteorites, sand from the African deserts . . . and even dinosaur bones.

Now is then.

What you see right now isn't necessarily what's
happening right now.

There's so much visual information arriving from the world around you that your brain needs time to process it all—and to filter out the unimportant stuff. How much time? More than you think: up to 10–15 seconds . . . which means that some of the things you think you're seeing right now may have actually happened 15 seconds ago. Research shows that your brain pieces together "snapshots" of the world every 10–15 seconds and "averages" the information into the smooth, flowing image that we consider "now."

The paradox of perception

The sky looks like a vast blue expanse above you. But it's not really blue ... and it's not really above you.

We *live* in the sky. It actually starts at your feet—not over your head—and extends all the way up to somewhere between the Kármán Line (about 67 miles up), where the atmosphere becomes too thin to support aeronautical flight, and, well, forever. As you can see, the sky directly around you isn't blue. And it isn't blue 67 miles up, either. But from a distance it *appears* blue because of a phenomenon called "light scattering." What you perceive as the blue of the sky is actually sunlight scattered by the tiny molecules of air as it passes through the atmosphere. Blue/violet light, which has a shorter wavelength than other colors, is scattered more than longer wavelengths of light. So more of it hits your eyes, which is why we see a blue sky.

What about other colors of the sky? When the Sun is low in the sky, such as at sunrise or sunset, the sunlight we see passes through more atmosphere than when the Sun is directly overhead. More blue light is scattered away, leaving the yellow, red, and orange wavelengths that give sunrises and sunsets their color.

Death is the beginning.

Looking for life in all the wrong places?

If you've never noticed dead trees while you're walking through a forest, you're missing something special: life. Studies show that there's more life in a dead tree than in a living one. In fact, 20 percent of Earth's plant and animal species depend on dead wood. That includes everything from fungi and bacteria to insects, worms, birds, and even the tree's own offspring, which feed off the parent tree as it decays and re-enriches the soil in a constant cycle of death, decomposition, and renewal.

Nothing you're made of is "you."

Every atom in your body existed before you did.

Think about it. If you took away the iron
in your blood, the calcium in your bones,
the water in your tissues, would you still be
human? Nope. You're the sum of your parts.
They can exist without you . . . but you can't
exist without them. And yet, they aren't you.

You really are attractive.

In fact, you exert a gravitational pull on everything around you.

Any matter that has mass also has gravity. That means everything on Earth is pulling on you right now—the Rocky Mountains, the carrots in your refrigerator, the Eiffel Tower, this book. But it also means you're attracting them. "Thus," as one scientist puts it, "when an apple falls to Earth, the Earth also falls to the apple." How far? "About one ten-millionth of the size of a proton." The attraction is very, very slight . . . but it's one more way that everything in the universe is connected.

Look up . . .

. . . on a clear night you can easily see 15 quadrillion miles.

You may not have super-vision, but there's no real limit to how far you can see. As long as the light emanating from an object hits the retinal cells in your eye, you can see it. On a clear night, for example, you can see a star called Deneb, about 15,000,000,000,000,000 miles away. (That's 15 *quadrillion*.)
And if conditions are just right, you can spot the star Eta Carinae with your naked eye. Eta Carinae is 45 quadrillion miles away.

All one family

Blue eyes appeared as a genetic mutation in one
person, 6,000–10,000 years ago.

Everyone with blue eyes today is descended
from that person.

What is the night?

The Earth's shadow.

Earth's shadow is always there, extending almost a million miles into space. As our planet rotates, we slip into its shadow every sunset—in fact, at twilight, we can actually see it approaching. Eventually, the planet blocks the Sun's light entirely, and we experience what we call night.

Just passing through

Right now, hundreds of trillions of solar
neutrinos are passing through your body.

Neutrinos are subatomic "ghost particles,"
formed in the nuclear reactions of stars like
our Sun. They have almost no mass and no
electric charge and travel through space at
near light speed, passing through matter as
easily as we move through air. To neutrinos
you are transparent. Indoors or outdoors, day
or night, trillions are always passing through
you . . . and you never know it.

How thin . . .

. . . is the atmosphere?

Imagine getting in your car and driving 12 miles straight up. At 65 mph, it would take only 11 minutes to get through the troposphere—the part of our atmosphere that contains all our weather, all our oxygen, and all that keeps us alive. To put it another way, if the Earth were the size of a Ping-Pong ball, the atmosphere would be no thicker than a layer of paint.

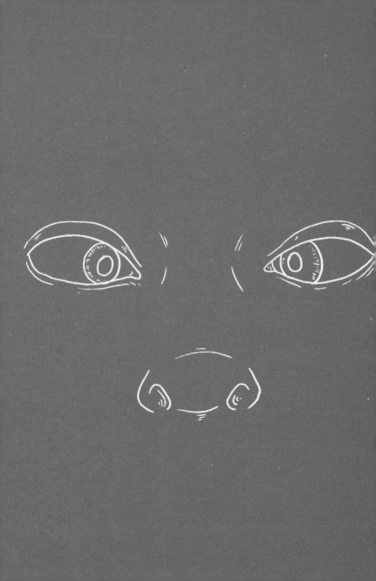

Can you . . .

. . . see your nose?

Check it out: If you close one eye, you can see your nose clearly. But if you look out of both eyes, it disappears. Why? Because your brain "automatically" ignores any information it doesn't consider important. And apparently your nose is one of those things. You rarely see it, even though it's in plain sight.

Everything is connected.

Because ice cubes float, fish live.

Most liquids become denser and heavier as they cool. But water is different. By the time it freezes, it's about 9 percent less dense than when it was liquid, which means it floats—unlike most other frozen liquids. The result: Ponds freeze from the top down—not from the bottom up—and aquatic life in freezing climates can survive under the ice instead of being frozen by it.

Magnetic power

Earth's magnetic field prevents the Sun from
exterminating you . . . and all life on the planet.

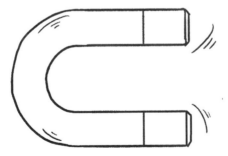

"Solar wind" sounds like two good things in one—sunshine and wind. But it actually refers to the stream of deadly electrically charged particles traveling from the Sun at speeds of up to a million miles per hour. If they ever struck Earth at full force, the atmosphere would be stripped away and all life would end. In fact, scientists speculate that this is what happened to Mars. But we're protected by Earth's magnetic field. It creates an invisible shield around us that extends thousands of miles into space and deflects the solar wind, making it go *around* our planet "like water around a ship's bow."

A few particles do make it past the magnetic field, though. They collide harmlessly with the atmosphere and provide us with the northern and southern lights.

You . . .

. . . are an ecosystem.

More than one, in fact. Your skin, your mouth, your stomach, and every part of your body that comes in contact with the outside world have their own unique communities of microbes. Many of these "alien" life-forms are with you from birth; you acquire the rest by the time you're three. Each body part is a village or an island unto itself: your left hand, for example shares only a sixth of its microbial species with your right hand. That's because the skin on one hand is drier, or sweatier, or oilier than the other hand, allowing different species of microbes to thrive. And it's not just your hands—it's every part of your body. Even each tooth in your mouth is host to its own unique combination of microbes.

Your cells are vastly outnumbered by these outside life-forms. If that sounds scary, keep in mind that a lot of them are necessary to your well-being. They fight inflammation, aid digestion, help produce amino acids that your body can't produce, and fight off harmful invading microbes. You are more than just an individual, you are a superorganism coexisting with trillions of other life-forms. You wouldn't be healthy—or human—without them.

Stand up.

Are you pushing down on the floor . . . or is the floor pushing up at you?

Both. If the floor weren't pushing you, you'd fall right through it. And if you weren't pushing back with an equal force, you'd get launched into the air. When you lean on a wall, it's leaning on you.
When you put your elbow on a table, the table is pushing back. If you're sitting in a chair right now, your butt and the chair are pushing each other with an equal force . . . and you have that relationship with all of the objects in your world.

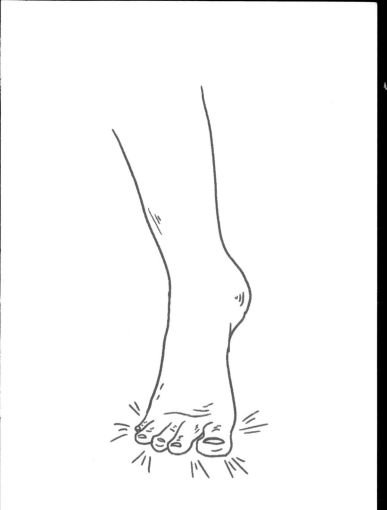

How much...

...of the Sun's total energy actually
reaches us every day?

Only 0.00000005 percent (that's 50
billionths of 1 percent). But it's still enough
to maintain all life on the planet. To put it in
perspective: This tiny fraction of the Sun's
daily light is about equal to the amount of
energy stored in the world's entire nuclear
arsenal.

Nothing you're made of is "you."

Every atom in your body existed before you did.

Think about it. If you took away the iron in your blood, the calcium in your bones, the water in your tissues, would you still be human? Nope. You're the sum of your parts. They can exist without you . . . but you can't exist without them. And yet, they aren't you.

Make a cup of tea . . .

. . . and you're releasing oxygen that was
breathed by creatures 100 million years ago.

The water you boil to make your morning
cup of tea or coffee probably contains
minerals, because groundwater percolates
through limestone before it's pumped from
the ground. Some of this limestone dissolves
into the water, only to reappear as "scale" on
the walls of your coffeemaker or teakettle.
That limestone is the remnant of skeletons of
plankton and other tiny ocean creatures who
lived more than 100 million years ago.

Those skeletons also captured oxygen from
the period, so when you boil water, you
release the oxygen, in the process catching
a whiff of the same air that the creatures
breathed a long, long time ago.

You're star blind.

Stars don't "come out" at night—they're there all the time. You just can't see them.

On a sunny, cloudless day, the sky is 10 million times brighter than the blackest night. The light from the Sun dominates the sky, and our brains react by blending the tiny points of starlight reaching us from trillions of miles away with the bright blanket of sunlight that has traveled "only" 93 million miles.

How fast . . .

. . . does a word travel?

Here's one way your words have power—they leave your mouth at 740 miles per hour, the speed of sound (also known as *Mach 1*). Your breath, on the other hand, only comes out at about five miles per hour.

A river runs through you.

While you're reading this, your body is leaking water.

You probably think of yourself as a sealed package, but you're actually quite porous; water flows out of you constantly. Because your mouth and lungs are moist, for example, every breath you exhale contains water vapor. And your 2–4 million sweat glands are steadily at work eliminating moisture through your skin. "This exchange of water molecules between you and the atmosphere," writes science journalist Curt Stager, "means that you are more or less continuous with your surroundings."

Beauty is fleeting.

Need proof? Just look at the night-blooming cereus.

The "queen of the night" is an unassuming cactus that's native to the deserts of northern Mexico. Most of the time the plant is inconspicuous—it looks like a dead bush. But once every year, as night falls on a summer evening, its beautiful, fragrant flowers open. The blooms last only until morning, though: When the Sun's first rays appear, the petals wilt and die.

The smell of the earth

That aroma you love is not what it seems to be.

That fresh aroma in the air after a rainstorm isn't the smell of the rain, nor is it the smell of air that's been washed clean of pollution. What you're actually smelling are chemicals like *geosmin*, a compound secreted by bacteria and fungi during reproduction. The chemicals accumulate in the soil during dry conditions and gets launched into the air when raindrops splash onto the ground.

Measuring the universe

How far away is the Moon?

The Moon is the closest celestial body to Earth . . . and it's still more than 238,000 miles away. That's so far from us that every planet in our solar system, including Pluto, could fit between Earth and the Moon. The Moon keeps getting farther away. Scientists speculate that when it was first formed, the Moon was just 14,000 miles from Earth.

Perfect balance

You . . . and the air around you.

The pressure inside your body is perfectly balanced with the pressure of the atmosphere, which is why you aren't being crushed by the air around you (or expanding into the next room).

Inner space

There are more living creatures in your mouth
than there are people on Earth.

Your mouth is a lush jungle that's home to
billions of microbes. In fact, researchers have
discovered more than 600 different species
of bacteria living in human mouths.

All one family

Fish use tools.

Until about 60 years ago, scientists were sure that only humans could use tools—and they regarded it as an example of how we're different from *all* other animals. But that notion has been turned on its head. Since then, for example, we've learned that chimpanzees use stones as hammers and anvils; gorillas use walking sticks; ravens make their own toys; octopuses use coconut shells for shelter; elephants make water vessels to drink from. And in 2011, a diver photographed a blackspot tuskfish smashing clamshells against rocks to get at the clams inside—proof that fish use tools, too.

Inner space

There's more of you than you think.

The surface area of your gastrointestinal system is about equal to the size of a studio apartment.

Loneliness of space

Feeling big? You're actually pretty small.

How empty is space? "The fastest most of us have traveled is 500 mph, the speed of a jet," says one scientist. "If we set out for the nearest star beyond our solar system at that speed, it would take about five million years to reach our destination." To put it another way, if you traveled in the fastest rocket ship ever made on Earth, the trip would still take more than 79,000 years—roughly a thousand human life spans.

I am you and
you are me.

When you see someone smile, your brain smiles
back at them.

When you smile, certain neurons in your brain are activated as part of the process. They're also activated when you see someone *else* smile. These cells are called "mirror neurons" because they mirror the behavior of others as if it were your own. Other sets of mirror neurons fire when you reach for an object, wave at a friend, or curl up your nose when you smell something awful. That's what enables you to interpret the gestures, facial expressions, and body language of other people and enables others to understand you.

You . . .

. . . are mostly empty space.

Your entire body is made of atoms. But only about 1 percent of every atom is matter (protons, neutrons, and electrons). The rest is empty space.

To get an idea of how empty that is, imagine that the smallest atom in your body (a hydrogen atom) was half a mile wide. The nucleus—which contains most of the atom's mass (the protons and neutrons)—would still only be the size of a marble in the center.

To put it another way: If the empty space in all atoms were removed, the entire human race would fit in the volume of a sugar cube.

What's up?

Bugs—billions of them.

You can't see the millions of bugs flying and floating above you. But they're there. It's an invisible highway in the sky, where an estimated one trillion insects pass overhead during the year.

They're the same bugs that inhabit your airspace: moths, beetles, flies, and spiders. There are more of them in summer, but it has been estimated that at any time, there are 25 million bugs in the air over every temperate square mile on the planet, in a column that extends up for thousands of feet. (One termite was captured at 19,000 feet—a record altitude.)

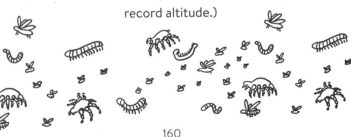

You're in the dark.

Your brain gives you sight, but it exists in complete darkness.

When light enters your eyes and strikes the light-sensitive cells in the retina, your optic nerve sends electrical signals to your brain . . . which interprets the signals as visual images. But the light never travels any farther than your retina. Despite the fact that it gives you sight, your brain will live in complete darkness forever.

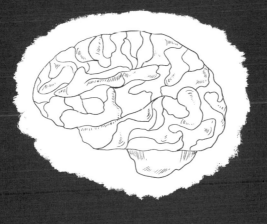

Improbable planet

Water is the most abundant compound in the universe, but it exists as a liquid in very few places in our solar system. Luckily, Earth is one of them.

We take liquid water for granted, but we shouldn't: It's a marvel. Temperatures in space range millions of degrees—from -385°F on the Moon, for example, to 15 million°F on the Sun. For Earth to have liquid water, the planet's temperature has to be consistently between the extraordinarily specific range of 32°F (when it freezes and becomes a solid) and 212°F (when it boils and turns into a gas). There are very few places in the universe where that is true. In fact, scientists are sure of only one: Earth.

Can plants . . .

. . . talk to each other?

They don't have the power of speech, but . . .
yes, they communicate with each other. For
example: Some plants release a "warning"
scent into the air when insects attack them.
Other plants in the area receive the message
somehow and produce chemicals that
make them less appetizing to invaders. And
some trees release electrical and chemical
distress signals through their roots when
attacked. This "distress call" is picked up by
nearby plants, which use the information as a
trigger to start making insecticide to defend
themselves. It's even been reported that in
some cases, parent plants will send nutrients
and provide drought protections to their
offspring.

All one family

Like you, elephants grieve for their dead.

African elephants are one of the few species that spend any time with the remains of their dead. There are numerous accounts of elephants standing in a circle around a recently deceased member of their group and stroking elephant bones with their trunks— even when they don't belong to members the same pack. (And they can distinguish between the bones of elephants and other large mammals.) Elephants have also been observed to cover their dead with leaves or dirt, making them the only mammals (other than humans) to perform burials.

Measuring the universe

How big is a speck of dust?

One speck of house dust is about halfway in size between a subatomic particle and the planet Earth.

You . . .

. . . are unconscious.

Well, most of you is, anyway. Scientists
estimate that we're unaware of as much as 98
percent of our brain activity—from automatic
actions like keeping our hearts beating and
digesting food to "adaptive consciousness,"
which applies to things like balance, language,
and decision-making. So if you think you know
what you're doing, you're probably only about
2 percent right.

The paradox of perception

You don't actually see things.

In ancient times, scientists thought beams
of light emanated from people's eyes and
illuminated the world. But your eyes are
really just receivers. You point them in a
direction, and they receive the band of
visible light that's either reflected off an
object or produced by one (such as a candle,
a lightbulb, or the Sun). You never see the
object itself—just the light.

Feel the flow.

You're part of a chain reaction that began at the birth of the universe . . . and will continue forever.

In a way, everything you've ever done is still happening, only in a different form. That's because no energy you expend ever disappears—it just moves from you to some other place. The first law of thermodynamics (one of the cornerstones of science) says that no energy is ever created or destroyed— all energy has always been here. Your energy came from somewhere else, which came from somewhere else, which came from . . . well, you get the point. Everything you do is a link in the chain reaction that began in the first moment, and all the energy that passes through you will continue until the universe ends.

Are you on solid ground?

Nope. Wherever you stand, Earth is shifting beneath your feet.

"Solid" ground isn't as solid as you think. The tectonic plates that make up Earth's crust fit together like pieces of a puzzle, and those pieces are constantly moving toward or away from each other. Fortunately, they aren't moving much—as little as a couple of millimeters a year—but it's another way you're always moving . . . even when you're standing still.

You will die . . .

. . . and that makes you lucky.

For you to die, you had to have been born in the first place—which, statistically speaking, is mind-bogglingly improbable.

Consider, first of all, that all the elements that make up your body parts have been "dead" for most of the last 13 billion years and had to come together in a very precise way to become "you." Then factor in the idea that over the last 3.8 billion years, as Bill Bryson writes, "every one of your forebears on both sides has been attractive enough to find a mate, healthy enough to reproduce, and sufficiently blessed by fate and circumstances to live long enough to do so."

As the scientist Richard Dawkins has observed, the moment before you were conceived, your consciousness was trillions of times less probable that it became a split second later. And even then there was no guarantee you would be born . . . or that you would survive long enough to be reading these words.

So yes, you are one of the lucky ones.

Acknowledgments

Our thanks to Max Hittesdorf for his inspiration, affirmation, explanations, information verification, imagination, exploration, confirmation, and good vibrations; to John Johnson and Mike Vediner for sharing their passion for science and their knowledge of physics; and to our teammate John Dollison for his literary contributions.

Dedicated to our dear sister, Lorrie Bodger, who never saw this book, but would have loved it.

Running Press
Hachette Book Group
1290 Avenue of the Americas, New York, NY 10104
www.runningpress.com
@Running_Press

Printed in China

First Edition: February 2018

Published by Running Press, an imprint of Perseus Books, LLC, a subsidiary of
Hachette Book Group, Inc. The Running Press name and logo is a trademark of
the Hachette Book Group.

The Hachette Speakers Bureau provides a wide range of authors for speaking
events. To find out more, go to www.hachettespeakersbureau.com or call (866)
376-6591.

The publisher is not responsible for websites (or their content) that are not
owned by the publisher.

Illustrations copyright © 2018 by Baily Watro
Print book cover and interior design by Joshua McDonnell.

Library of Congress Control Number: 2017959770

ISBNs: 978-0-7624-6173-8 (hardcover), 978-0-7624-6174-5 (e-book)

1010

10 9 8 7 6 5 4 3 2 1